Slivers of Lost Light

poems by

Carlos Martinez

Finishing Line Press
Georgetown, Kentucky

Slivers of Lost Light

ACKNOWLEDGMENTS

In the matter of touch appeared in Noisy Water: An Anthology Of Poetry From
Whatcom County, Washington, 2015.

My most profound gratitude goes to Alexandra Beemsterboer. She did the
overwhelmingly major part in putting this collection together. Any, and all,
praise accrues to her. Any failures of this book are wholly and totally mine.

Publisher: Leah Maines

Editor: Christen Kincaid

Cover Art: Public Domain CC0

Author Photo: James Emilio Martinez

Cover Design: Elizabeth Maines McCleavy

Printed in the USA on acid-free paper.
Order online: www.finishinglinepress.com
also available on amazon.com

Author inquiries and mail orders:
Finishing Line Press
P. O. Box 1626
Georgetown, Kentucky 40324
U. S. A.

Table of Contents

IV.

For all of my beloved dead, who are my slivers of lost light: my mother and father, for Johnny and for Lori and for Ingrid.

For all of my beloved who are so alive: for Danny and Jamie and Elliot and Isaak, for the members of my family, and for Pat and for Denise, mothers of my children.

I.

Back from burying my father

Home at last, I open my front door, living
room dark, cats huddled on the couch,
or crouched in the room's far corners.
I stand still for a moment, reliving the dream
of the past week, heavy duffle bag
still gripped in my right hand . My father's
hands, how different they looked, folded
across his lap, than when, two weeks ago,
I held them as catheters went
in to help him pee, and how cold
his forehead when I bent to move his cap back
the undertaker put on him, to kiss
his brown skin caked with makeup, and how
still his chest, I'd hoped I would see move,
but didn't. I come in to my home, turn
a lamp on, and watch my cats stir, drifting
toward their bowls. It's as if
I had never left, thirteen hours there, eleven
hours back, to have sat in a viewing room, undertaker
looking like a wraith, a puff of moving smoke.

Slivers of lost light

For all of my elementary school classmates

Old, now, maybe dying or dead, those boys who once ran
across the concrete gymnasium floor beneath

the timeworn grammar school, where hoops hung askew
and the lines on the court had been almost erased

by athletic shoes—P F Flyers and Keds, Converse that were
considered stylish then—still bloom in time, and dribble and run

and shoot, smudged orange ball arcing into where
nets once hung. I, who never ran with them, too

clumsy and afraid, close my eyes to see them play, as I
did once, off to one side, trembling, book

clutched in one hand that I couldn't wait to get home to read.
Now, here, in this time, I sit at my desk

and lean back, closing my eyes to see those boys again, who
I haven't seen in years, rising, ball poised to be let loose.

[**Most mornings**]

Most mornings I write. Some mornings
I don't.

When I do, those poems
are filled with clichés having to do

with light and how it comes down,
shattering against shut blinds, or,

how when it slips through
cracks in them, it appears

to be sliced into ribbons
strewn

everywhere. In
those poems, there must always be

that first cigarette, the dawning
of that pleasure, the feeling

of lethal smoke wending its way down,
how magnificent that feels

before the first hacking cough.
There has to be coffee, dark and rich,

automatically brewed
while I still sleep, the aroma of it

drifting up the stairs
as I slowly descend, because

my old knees
aren't what they used to be. Any

processional move must appear to be
dignified, and not the product

of an incipient infirmity. Every poem
is about death. The appreciation of light

depends on its being a poem's subtext,
as does the appreciation of smoke

that swirls from my mouth
whenever I wheeze.

An elegy for when

On this year's Mother's Day

Let me try this morning to find a line with which
to begin, something about how, six years ago,
my mother died, going from warm to cool, from
pliable to stiff, or how a few months ago, lying
on his side, to keep his lungs drained of streaming
drool, my father's chest fell in. This morning, there is
no sun. Gray clouds, chill wind, reminding me
of winter months just passed, of having to bundle up
to go outside, even to smoke a cigarette, its smoke
frosting and falling to the ground. I grieve all of it,
everything, those deaths I've described, lost loves,
those women going away, their Facebook posts limning
new lives while I stay within four walls, wishing I had
a clock that didn't tick. I grieve my children growing up,
two already men, the silence of my phone, how its battery
 runs down without its ever going off. The youngest,
now six, I grieve for him as well, that when
I am gone, what then? Last night, I went to bed.
I slept and dreamed, riots of colors, pastel shades,
Technicolor streaks, the many voices I heard
and can neither forget nor recall. Coffee, cigarettes,
old cats whose morning hunger impels them to be
frantic, whirling balls when I descend my stairs to become
an old man to every mirror into which I will not look,
except an askance glance and, then, a turning.

Texas teen shoots and kills three-year old stepson for jumping on bed

There are those nights when you sleep through all of it, not even getting up
to go pee, though this is mitigated by the fact that you've had dream after dream
that can only be characterized as strange, even though you can't recall
even one of them in its entirety. All that remains are scraps and shards translucently
drifting back down to the floor of the basement of your mind, colors and sounds,
faces and isolated words, but you know everything in them was strange. You are
grateful, though, to have made it through another night, to have woken, bleary-eyed
and in some pain, your back really hurting, your legs, as well, and your bladder,
it feels as big as the Hindenburg about to explode. Nonetheless, to have
your eyes open, for consciousness to rise like some fetid creature mired in
swamp water, dripping and covered with slime end rotting vegetation, is, you think,
a gift and a blessing. The routine is the usual one, the graceless hobble to
the bathroom, to empty out, head thrown back, groan and sigh combined, and,
then, down the stairs, slowly, railing tightly gripped, so as not to succumb
to gravity's inexorable pull. Your grandmother went that way, down stairs
and through some metaphorical hole in the floor, and onward, or downward to
the somewhere else everyone eventually goes to. Cats to be fed, cigarette to be lit
and smoked outside, those first and most delicious puffs of the day, nicotine high,
then back in, to turn the computer on and get down to the business of manufacturing
a working mind again, bit by bit, piece by piece, shards retrieved and put
next to each other, and, when the order is right, glued by the mucilage of self.
Coffee, and lots of it, cup after cup downed, hot with the power to revive, and you,
saying to yourself over and over again *Lazarus rise Lazarus rise*, as you skim
poetry websites, sites where camgirls awake for hours are already furnishing
the world of single and lonely men the utmost delectation of their private selves,
and, then, on to news sites and news magazines where events both big and small
are displayed—the purported death of a Taliban leader by drone strike, the latest
outrage by a presidential candidate and what it was he said, the state of the world's
vanishing species of bear, fish, you name the creature, it's on its way out, and,
the last, the headline on a story you will read, but not just yet.

Get better

For my father, d. 29 Feb. 2016

As if that exhortation ever worked, as you lay in your bed,
in your hospital room, where the silent wraiths of RNs
and various specialized techs, and the two guys whose job
was to come in twice a week, to strip you out your robe,
and to roll you this way and that, hanging on so you
wouldn't fall from bed to floor, while they sponged
your old man's slack skin, and then dried you and dressed
you, to make you stand up, old hands gripping the railing
of a walker, to walk you ten paces down the hall, ten paces
back, walked in and out, taking your temperature, or
changing your diaper whenever you pushed your call button
because you had wet yourself one more time. I remember
their impassive faces, chiseled and carved, I was sure, while
they walked down to your room from their central station,
and how their jaws creaked when they opened their mouths
to say *Stay still* or *Does this hurt*, as if those words
were moths fluttering towards light before disappearing.
Those two words I spoke to you when I leaned down
to kiss your forehead and to squeeze your hand, clear signals
I was about to walk out, into my own life, leaving yours
far behind, beneath florescent light, and your eyes, I was sure,
scorching and scoring my back, the laser of your desire
to live longer cutting through my shirt and undershirt, through
layers of skin and nerve, my heart left charred.

Two days before Christmas

Last night
I dreamt

my sons
lined up to ask me

how many days
I have left?

How many? How many
hours and minutes

of sitting on the couch
wondering

when
my son's will call

or come visit,
or me

rubbing my head
wondering

when the rest of my hair
will fall?

After the morphine wears off and before the next dose

He notices
the lights aren't the kind he likes,
aren't his, shed
light too soft and fuzzy,
wonders why
the wrong music is playing,
not the *merengues*
or *plenas* of his youth, when
he'd take his shirt off
and danced in flickering fire light, beneath
palm trees, on white sand,
to the call of the *couqi*,
and where
might he be, in what
kind of bed, with covers
that aren't his, and
not enough of them,
and where
might his war medals be,
not hanging to his right
as he had them,
and his favorite easy chair,
almost worn through,
springs in it bent
by his years of sitting.
Why is it his legs won't move,
and why
is pain growing in his stomach, mouth
to dry to call out, and where
is his nightstand. Where 's
his phone. Where
are his god damned shoes.

1 Merengues and plenas are kinds of Latin dance music and the coqui is a small indigenous frog, a national symbol of Puerto Rico. The sound it makes
sounds likeits name

How I pray to our beloved lord
After Mary Szybist

Our Father, where the hell were you when you were needed,
during the ten months your most devout believer lay intubated,
strapped to her hospital bed, those leg cuff compression things
squeezing her blood upwards to her heart that burned the same say
your son's did in those old pictures of him with his heart
exposed for our veneration. And, where were you when our old man
found out about his T-cell lymphoma and had to be kept drugged
and out of it so that the pain did not feel like he was being pressed
up against the seething inferno of hell's hot gates. I held his hand,
so smooth for someone who had once been a working man, hauling
hawsers as thick as his leg and standing watch on the prows of ships
tossed by Poseidon's fury, who, I assume, was you, too. Where
were you then, when my father rose from his morphine coma
murmuring *No No Not yet*. Where were you the night my blind,
profoundly retarded cousin, just fourteen years old, rose from his bed
and went to feel his way to the bathroom, to pee or shit, who knows,
and sat and had his heart swell and explode, found dead the next morning,
in rigor and gray and cold. Where were you all of those times
when we needed you, who is said to reside in a parallel dimension,
one outside of our seeing, whose arms—you are said to have them—
are open in love and warmth. Where have you been all of the cold
and all of the too hot nights when my sister-in-law, your lover,
lay in her hospital bed, in her living room, fifty-six (don't you think
that's kind of young) groaning because of her pancreatic cancer until
the morning her chest rose high and then forever fell.

On the deaths by gunfire of Alton Sterling and Philando Castile

All night long, all over America, as the rest of us slept and dreamt,
others felt flame, felt fire rising up, felt fire coming out, the sound
of flame being made, their bodies wrapped in flame, burning,
dancing to whatever tune fire plays as it engulfs a body, as in
this case, the latest two, who had dreamt the night before,
both of them, dreams lit by thoughts of many years to come,
of laughter, of holding and being held, of many meals, savored
and thought about, of simple pleasures—of peeing, of walking
along in sun and rain, of waking, a kind of coming back. No more
coming back for them, eaten by fire that came, that was spat.
Now, those alive, who knew them, spin as if on fire themselves,
lost in grief's vast conflagrations, nothing like the flame that took
those two, looking up to see fire descending into them. How that
must have felt, to have felt those fires, skin split, bone shattered
by fire's swift passage.

An old friend stuck in a nursing home

There is where she feared having to appear, as if on command, as if
on command by powers unknown, by voices not heard yet compelling

her to be taken into the gloom, green walls, bad lighting, intermittently
flashing florescent bars in ceilings not high enough, hospital beds

occupied by who knows how many generations of those about to be dead
having come through them, dumped onto their old mattresses, turned

this way and that, wiped clean, medicated, ignored when they cried too loudly,
and, after having passed in the night, whisked down a hall and away to where

their disposal became someone else's responsibility. All night, she says,
someone down the hall howls, and she hears all times of day quavering

and high-pitched voices calling for help. No wonder she's feeling herself
shrink, deeper beneath washed-thin sheets, threadbare blanket, just one,

though she would like to have more, at least another one. She's asked
and watched a nurse's aide turn away, back to her, going through a door

to wherever the poorly paid gather to wash human shit and piss
from their hands. Crying in the night, shouting during the day

doesn't bother them, dressed in their scrubs, who drift from room to room
to check how everything's going. If, she says, these people were once lamps

whose bright glow illumined them into smiling, their guttering flames
blown out a long time ago by life and their employment. She's afraid,

she says, wonders why her speech patterns have all changed so that her words
now slur, smears in air she can barely inhale.

In the matter of touch
For my brother Emil

I have touched you in so many ways. First,
the touch of an older brother for a brother
just born, needing to be held and fed, to be
changed and carried from room to room,
needing the touch of words made smooth
and soothing. And, I have loved you in
the ways older brothers love younger ones,
with pinches and wedgies, open-palmed
slaps to the back of your head, hard, but not
too hard, not enough to do more than sting,
to leave a glow of pain behind briefly, to let
you know who was in charge, who not. And,
when you were older, enough to understand,
I used my fists, but weakly, again, to not
cause damage that would last, hit you because
how else can one brother express love to
another brother, whose face was always
tilted slightly up, expectant and smiling,
thinking, I'm sure, behind your brown eyes,
there was something I was trying to say
that wouldn't come out as perfectly shaped
as I had wanted, that words drip and fall
and are swept away, meaning nothing. Now,
after your wife's funeral, I have come
to touch you again, an old man on a sidewalk
with one of his younger brothers, my arms thin,
flesh sagging from them, to fold them around you,
squeezing you as hard as I could.

The precocious 7-year old prays for the resurrection of his blind, retarded cousin
For Johnny, 14, d. 1957

You did it once. Come down and do it again.
Come from behind the clouds where you hide, when

we come to your house to kneel and feel hard wood bruise,
the discomfort that your love requires, small thing

compared to your time spent nailed to that cross, where
you hung till dead. You came back again, and I know

you felt love for everything here, for every bush
and grain of sand beneath your sandals, for every small

creature scurrying outside of where you stayed. I know
you loved every sunbaked man and woman, loved them

enough to go willingly, though you knew that for you,
dead was not dead. My cousin lies in front of me, stiff, still,

his chest no longer going up and down. I know enough
to know he hasn't had oils and perfumes smeared across him,

that he is filled with who knows what chemicals, to keep him
the way he now appears. I kneel in front of him to ask this—

Bring him back. Come out from wherever it was you went,
rising until out of sight, leaving those who loved you filled

with awe and wonderment. I ask you now to come down,
to put your hands on my cousin's hard skin, whose only sins

were being blind and not all there, who knew enough
to love you as much as I have. Help him and me. Place

your pierced hand on his chest. Allow me to witness
his first inhalation after his death, and help me help sit him up,

his green eyes opened and seeing, his mind, that was never really there, made as whole as it always should have been.

Recuperation

For a friend, in the hospital after surgery and before her death

I will finger the scar along my sternum most nights, will touch it
while I wait for another program to come on, recalling the feel
of staples—or was it stitches—the way those felt being removed,
pulled out or cut, the sound of small scissors snipping or of what
mechanism remove staples from humans who feel as if reports
to be recycled. They nights they say are long, are just long enough
for me to look at a ceiling, and to close my eyes but not sleep,
long enough for me to use my imagination, as if it could be a net
I throw forward in time, to catch whatever events may happen,
that I may drag back to the moment where I am, for my inspection.
I'm not familiar with the within doctors become intimate with
when that colonoscopy was done, and a doctor bent over and peered
into me, shining a light where the sun never shone, to make sure
nothing lurked or grew, to surprise me when I did not expect
my body to nail a manifesto of its discontent to my heart. Now,
I lie in a room recovering, waiting for a therapist to come through
the door, shedding light, all of it artificial, florescent, not the warm
yellow light of fires and incandescent bulbs, now forever banned,
a young man or woman who do not understand how time grinds
on cartilage, wears through walls of muscles, make of red blood
cells, thin spinning platters a magician cannot keep spinning
on his stick forever. I wait for young nurses, who cannot
understand that where I am, where I lie, who I've become
seems to have happened in just an instant, that I am who they
will someday turn into, surprised at the ambulance showing up
at their doors, to carry them from home, the way light in homes
is different than light anywhere else, into places where light comes
from ceiling fixtures, the glare of it never dimmed. I wait for someone
who may remember they love me to come through the door, carrying
a bouquet of inexpensive flowers, bunched and ready to go, bought
on the way to come spend five or ten minutes before vanishing
through what seems less door, more time portal, wormhole back
into normal life. I wait for a tray of hospital food—sickly chicken
leg covered with a sheen of grease, instant mash potatoes, tea or
coffee, a dwarf carton of chocolate milk, a plastic cup filled with Jello,
the consistency of the vessel within which I still live.

The secret lives of skin cancers

Outside into it is what you say you cannot do, into
sunlight when it is out and strong, its rays to turn you
bright red your fair Swedish skin, so that you are forced
to stay inside, or to cover every inch of you, floppy
hats with wide brims down over your eyes. You want
to avoid wrinkling, puckering, trips to doctors who tell you
of the dangers of keloid scarring, of growths that bud, as if
all that you kept secret within yourself, sprouts and grows,
polyps growing into other versions of who you are—evil,
angry, the one whose hunger for sex cannot ever be satisfied.
If these were to grow, reaching maturity, your doctors say
they would overcome you, becoming melanomas, but
you suspect each one would pop off, dropping to
your bedroom floor in the middle of the night, birthed
in moonlight, its silver limning these new versions of who
you would have liked to have been, the sins you wanted
to commit, and you constrained by vows of fidelity and love,
motherhood's responsibilities, what your friends
would have thought.

My father's birthday

Ninety-three years ago this night,
somewhere in a thrown-together hut,
my father came out by firelight, from in between

his long-dead mother's legs, glistening
by guttering flame, and fell
into some dead woman's hands, who

wrapped him in old rags. He cried,
was placed on either rags or straw,
was held, was fed. I imagine everything

in that orange light, the way it moved,
the way it swayed, the grunts
my father's mother made, to have him

slide slowly out. Now, in his room,
in his empty house, wife dead, children grown,
old pictures on his walls—of wife, of children

when they were young—he sits
in an old rocking chair, revisiting his life—
years of hunger, years at war, years at sea,

on the prows of ships, his coming home,
a stranger. One light on, one small lamp
flickers as he sits and waits.

II.

Refrain

Now, I wear my father's watch,
he for whom time has stopped.
In his tomb, there is no clock.
Now, I wear my father's watch,
he for whom time has stopped.
In his tomb there is no clock,
he for whom time has stopped.
Now, I wear my father's watch.
I wait for it to stop.

The texture of regret

I can hear it whining clearly enough as it goes, not
as well lubricated as it should be, by a drink or two,
of wine or something stronger, or by a toke or two
from a badly-rolled joint, my mind, in the middle of
the night, thinking about my old lady who is gone,
not the one who died, who is nothing more, now,
than tissue paper in her tattered dress, but the one
who one day just got up and left, having had enough
of arrogance and certitude, the blazing of it
from my forehead and chest, puffed out. How thrilled
I once was at having been born myself, and how
I had become the man I was, how tall and thin, how
distinguished-looking and professorial, until the day
she walked through the door, and it seemed as if
she had not even bothered opening it. Those days,
how halcyon they now seem, when she was here,
near to me at night, and when we made love, how
we both looked, reflected in the mirror on the dresser,
where we could be ourselves, the way our faces looked
as we came then fell on our backs and listened to
the peregrinations of our neighbors
transiting the parking lot where we would go,
sedate and calm, afterwards. They say nights are long,
alone, in the dark, listening to the Doppler gods
speeding to and fro, one forearm resting on
one's wrinkled forehead, one hand between one's legs,
for comfort, and as an aid to remembering what was,
and then, as the poets say, a trip along the Lethe,
the length of it, and, of course, dreams in which
everything goes wrong, or everything is fixed and well,
all right enough that delight springs up, and just
before waking, the urge to laugh out loud is strong,
and then waking happens. So many years ago, now,
she left, packing everything of hers, leaving behind
every gift, every shining trinket, every token given,
those she wore and those she kept put away, left

strewn on bed and floor, on kitchen counter and along
the couch's full length.

[Why do we men assume there is an allure]

Why do we men assume there is an allure
to our penises, irresistible members jutting out,

when, excited, we remove it from out pants,
bringing it from constraint and humid dark,

sometimes fetid, having its own aromas, we
bring it into light, in our cars, at the end

of a night—dinner, drinks, or at a movie,
afterwards—slipping it from its hiding,

allowing it to wave, upright. Why do we
men think it's all right to show it to a woman,

who, we hope, will promptly fall upon it,
taking it into her mouth, enveloping it

with a hand, smooth palm, prelude to
placing it within herself while looking into

our eyes, that brim with hope, with desire,
with a need, to empty ourselves of semi-replicas

of who we are, hoping another one of us
does not take shape or become. Date after date,

end of night after end of night, it pushes
against imprisoning clothes, hoping

that we listen to its pleas—*Let me out
Let me out.*

Poem for someone who wouldn't want it

I dreamt the past was never past redeeming...
Richard Wilbur

This night, this day, which doesn't matter, somewhere in
a room, blinds shut, curtains drawn, and, if there's a shade,

that's pulled down, too, you lie in a private place,
within my skull, where doors exist to go through, deeper

into what was never said, where I imagine you lie on your bed, nude,
graceful, fleshy, fat, replete, full, gorgeous in the same way

a ball of light far away in darkness, beckoning to someone
who became lost, is beautiful. That is to say, you are a beacon,

or have become so to me, fanciful, wishful, limned by a wanting
to remember in one particular way, not imperfections nor

defects in character and outlook, but the woman once captured in
photographs, giving off a radiance beyond the power of language

to adequately outline, a need to understand. Oh, love, or,
once love, now stranger whose familiar face looms whenever

I blink, in that brief moment, filled with that particular look
someone in love wears, as you did once, I see you.

Slivers of lost light II

After Joanna Solfrian

Now that the children are grown and gone, and I'm divorced, and all that stays
are all of the old photographs on the walls, of them when young, and I go
from wall to wall, peering close, and hope for my cell phone to ring, from
a call from one of them coming in, or the simple ding, in an absolute vacuum
of silence, of a text ,message waiting to appear on my old flip phone's screen,
I stop and lean against cheap plasterboard, afraid it may collapse from weight
pressed against its thin molecules, and, wanting to be melodramatic, I pant
I groan, and raise my hands in front of my face, the better able to admire
the quality of crepe skin in evening light coming through the smudged window
on the landing between two floors, metaphor, I think, before I straighten a spine
that wants to bend, and stay that way, and grab the loose railing I am afraid
I may pull from its wall, and go down to where I will feel for the location of
old lamps, that sometimes seem to move on their own across the living room,
seeking spots where they might be left alone, when twilight comes.

Gladly becoming Darth Vader because it is required

Yesterday, my five-year old son sat in my lap for hours as we watched videos
on my computer screen, and I wrapped my arms around him, leaning in close
to more easily whisper in his ear how much I love him, words barely audible,

that he heard, leaning back. Afterwards, upstairs, I took one of his light sabers,
and leaped across my bed, and fell to the floor and rolled, and rose
into my evilness, my dark soul, and pretended I could not easily breathe,

and took, with good grace, every blow from his light saber and groaned and fell.
Do you have any idea how hard it is for a sixty-five year old man with bad knees
to leap across a bed, or to fall and leap lithely to his feet, wielding a weapon

that must slice air in a specific pattern, how much it hurts to roll over toys strewn
where they are not seen until one falls on them? The whole time the small
face of your child, who doesn't yet know what aging means or what delicacy

advancing through years eventually entails, who wants to do these acts
over and over, until ibuprofen, later, will not prove enough to mitigate the aches.
I jumped and rolled and flailed and ran from room to room, pursued, harried,

as it is appropriate for any totem of evil to be, his laughter behind me, the tip
of his sizzling blade millimeters from my spine. Afterwards, more videos,
a glass of chocolate milk for him. For me, remembering our going out to where,

once, an old woman came up to tell me what a beautiful grandchild I had,
to which I responded *Not my grandchild. My son.*

[Little daughter I never had]

Little daughter I never had, I rise each night to wander
down the hall, in the dark, stumbling on the toys I would
have given you, but never did. I open the door to what
would have been your room, where my six-year old son
keeps his toy strewn, and I do not see the mess he makes
when he comes from his mother's house to mine, the way
his toys are thrown around, lying alone or in heaps, stuffed
toys patiently waiting, waiting for his return, for his
small hands to pick them, to give them life. There is a life
you never had, never having been, nothing more than just
a wish, a dream, a desire to have held you in my arms
shortly after your birth, to have carried you on my back
to park and zoo, for walks in sun and rain. I look into
that room, where you should have been, and close my eyes,
opening them to see you, covers kicked off, back to me,
curled into yourself, the rise and fall of you as you breathe,
night light on and bright.

Couplets for my former wife, written toward the end of 2014

Last time you were in town, we got together for coffee, you looking not a day older
than on the day the judge handed down our divorce decree, except now, a wedding
    ring

with a large and sparkling diamond sits on your finger, a ring you wear comfortably,
as we sip and talk about what our sons have been up to, the vicissitudes of their
    growing up

and getting older, how they still get in trouble and sometimes cannot handle it.
We sip and all I can think of is how what I really want to do is not

lean across the table to plant a kiss on those lips I kissed so many times, but to go
outside, to have a cigarette and look at blue sky or down at the asses

of women crossing the parking lot. I try to imagine the man who now sleeps
next to you, and what it must be like for you to have his arms slip around you

as you make love and then fall asleep. You ask after me, what my life is like, and I
have so little to say, do not say how I rise when it is dark and walk alone toward the
    aroma

of coffee brewed while I slept, and how it seems like every day, it's become
a little harder to bend down to put my shoes on, to knot their laces, and how, when

I am alone at night, I see the many faces of past lovers, some dead, some, like you,
alive and gone, and wake with my arms stretched out to put them around

someone's absent shoulders. Instead, I say life's all right, that getting older,
what an interesting experience it's turning out to be.

Brief meditation on the notion of *Once*

Once, when once was a thing, and I was thin and could slide
across any kind of floor, from one room into another, through

any door, locked or unlocked, I could stand straight as I
slid, I sang, though my voice was too high for a man's and it

cracked, it broke, as each mended note fell from my tongue,
trail of crumbs I left behind to help me find my way back

to where I had once begun, because once was once, limned
in the beauty memory imparts, even those bad things, those

events sepia-colored, the brighter ones called up again
and made as shiny as a talisman or a coin repeatedly

brought forth and rubbed. I was once what I was and loved
being that being who came only once and then was gone, once

being a concept too alien to comprehend, that once happened
and that other instances of its happening were not it.

III.

Where have you gone, my once lovely faith
St. Paul's Church, Spanish Harlem

Back in those days, kneeling was a challenge,
in the Catholic church that was almost big enough
to have been a cathedral, but it never became, as
some planets, gaseous and huge, spinning as they do,
and growing hotter, never grow hot enough to become
actual stars, and glow dully in the firmament. Our
church was like that, stone glowing red at twilight,
cold and gray, a shade of it combined with what I
would call the color dun, and cold inside, even on
warm days, or at the height of summer, light filtered
by stained glass windows, shadows everywhere. I
went in to it too many times to count, from my
infancy, made wet on my forehead and thereby
absolved of the sin of having become. And, when,
I was old enough, I went in on Sundays, to listen to
a priest drone—to a child, that's what it sounded like—
in Latin, the glimmer of gold thread shot throughout
his vestments, the gold of his chalice, the gold
of the tabernacle where god was said to live. I knelt
on hard and splintering wood, worn
by generations before—the Irish, the Italians, their
little boys dragged to church, to kneel and fold
their hands, to pray to the god in the little gold house.
I knelt and prayed, asking god for his forgiveness,
for him to make sure my father, always at sea,
stayed safe, prayed for my mother, whose
incandescence as she cleaned and cooked and washed
dishes by hand, and scrubbed laundry in the kitchen
sink, might remain alive and safe, giving off the light
I knew I needed, and for my brothers and sisters,
our cat, our rabbit, our guinea pig and parakeet, our
fish, gold and otherwise, for our pet duck, the hamster,
for all of our dogs rescued from the pound. I prayed
the worn linoleum of our floor would wear out
no more, and that the refrigerator would always be full,
that the rats, and even the roaches might live long.

What came to mind this winter morning

After my mother died, and it came time
for her to be prepared, my sisters said
they'd do her hair the way she liked,
They went into a back room,
or down a flight of stairs, into wherever
she was kept, a place beyond
her children's imagining. When I asked
if I could help, if I could hold a comb
or brush, if I could help wash her hair,
my sisters said this was something
the women had to do.

The delivery of my sons via C-sections
For Pat and Denise, their mothers, and for Danny, Jamie, and Elliot

Oh, that morning, those mornings, still dark outside, the hallways
down which a gurney, or gurneys rolled, the sound of gurney wheels,
and, under thin sheets, wearing thin hospital gowns, the mothers,
separated in time, but women I loved, still loved, though time
and the expansion of the universe, even as we stand still, separates them
from me. Into the delivery rooms, beneath those bright, white lights
that might make anyone think heaven lay beyond them, the anesthesiologists
sitting on their stools, in front of their beeping machines, those machines'
blinking lights, green, red, blue, yellow. I remember it, the application
of gas to make those mothers, not fall asleep, but to appear to float,
first, a few inches above those operating tables, then a foot, their legs
opened, held open, doctors and nurses leaning in to see what I thought of
as the miracles. No children came forward, no heads crowned, no hair, wet
and glistening, destined to fall out before growing again, jutted into air.
I remember the sharp knives, the glitter of florescent light on short blades,
the breathing of all of us in that operating theater, the way we synchronized,
and, how for just a few moments, I thought of all of us, mothers, doctors,
nurses, myself as synchronized swimmers trying to win the gold. Pulled
from in between those two incised flaps of stomach skin, feet first, slick
with blood, gleaming with whatever remnants of amniotic fluid, my sons,
at different times, in different years, their curled bodies were pulled out
and held by their heels, dangling in air, their first cries coming together,
in my remembering, to become an a cappella song.

[How those red beans glistened]

What a shame she never wrote any of her recipes down.
A friend of my mother, at my mother's funeral

How those red beans glistened in her cast iron pot, blackened by years,
how steam rose from them, water boiling, water bubbling, as my mother,
her brown, old hands, stirred them, her children in her kitchen's doorway,

inhaling, drawing the aroma of those beans in, deep, eyes half-closed.
We swayed, all of us, as if about to faint, as we watched our mother move
around that pot, adding a pinch of this, a little of that. never measuring

any ingredient, and we thought about, we talked about it later, how
our mother seemed like a witch at her cauldron, steam the essence of
her magic, swirling its way toward heaven. Good witch, we told each other,

just witch, who took her children into her kitchen, not a cavern or an old
and dilapidated cottage exuding evil, but a space she almost never left,
too warm most days, a shelter in winter, where she stood after her cooking

was done, and beckoned us to come to her. We walked in single file, or,
sometimes, we became a mob, wanting to watch her fill our plates, rim
to rim, one side to the other, food as a manifest destiny spreading across

ceramic. We sat at her kitchen table, bent over, busily eating, and listened
to her behind us, scooping more of this, more of that, and we bent and ate
and thought of her, when our backs were turned, mesmerized by her food,

those red beans nestled into rice, next to pork chops that shone with grease
so brightly, we were blinded, next to plantain slices on the side, our mother,
always in the kitchen, who never stopped.

Blink and blink again and there is a memory
For my father

i.

The week before you died, I held your hand
while a technician slipped a catheter in, and felt
your weakened grip, and saw you wince, and I
was surprised at how soft your palm felt, the hand
of a man who had done manual work his whole life,
and when you died, embalmed and still, I saw
those hands folded, no longer alive, and how
they didn't look like they were yours, bruised
and black and blue along the top of them, and
I thought of that soft palm I gripped and held
one last time.

ii.

What this goes back to is this—when I was three,
my father, home from the sea, took me with him
for a run to the grocery store. As we walked down
Third Avenue—it was a rainy night and everything
was slick with just-fallen rain and glittering, as if
in Technicolor—I lost his grip on my hand and we
became separated, and those who are now
only wraiths in my memory, insubstantial and
shadowed, and walking along, came between us.

iii.

A little boy, all alone of a sudden, I panicked, feeling
that feeling of wild fear rise up, and looked for him.
Running up to a man as big as my father was, who
looked like him from behind, I grabbed a stranger's hand,
and found him looking down, perplexed. My father
appeared, laughing, and took my hand in his, that felt
hard and callused.

The East River

What was there in it to have been seen? Even on the cloudiest of days
it had a sheen to it, it was dirty, filled with flotsam—tin cans, old
milk containers, cardboard, shoes, overcoats and jackets, too, and,
once in a blue moon, someone dead, back humped up, bloated, floating
along with a dog, a cat, or a rodent, the kind that liked to enter
bedrooms at night to bite babies' toes, fast asleep. This was the river
not too far from home, a three-block walk, in late spring, or summertime,
to watch tugboats cruising by, Circle Line tour boats filled
with gawking tourists lounging against those ships' railings, like old clothes
hanging from laundry lines. There, on benches missing slats, grounded
in concrete, looking as ancient as ruins, I perched precariously, and looked
at Brooklyn's shoreline—wharves and piers, warehouses tilted seaward, emptied,
as if, at any moment, about to slip into that dark soup. Evenings, sometimes,
if not too afraid of walking home after dark, what might lurk in doorways, I went
    down
to where that water flowed from upstate New York and out to sea. I stood, alone,
on its banks, watching garbage floating by, and, being young, I dreamt.

My father breaks his silence

And, into those cold squalls, those old freighters plowed on, going up, down,
side to side, rolling, yawing, and there they all were, that crew—the Swede,
the Pakistani, the German, the one who spoke no known language, the mates, all
three of them, the captain in his wheelhouse, the rusted ship with its hold full, in
the time before containers, when cargo was loaded through hatches that creaked
     open,
slowly closed, smoke rising from the one stack way above, into storms, searing
     sun,
nights so cold and clear, those mariners told each other, each time a meteor flew
     over,
sizzling into salt water, god's finger scratching the sky. Once, my father told me,
there was a parrot one captain had, that never shut up, always talked and sang,
     day,
night, during every watch, and what was it about the acoustics of that ship, that
damned beautifully plumed bird—red, yellow and green—it could be heard
     everywhere, even in
the head, back when I didn't know a head was a bathroom and shower, and thought
its raucous words burrowed through those sailor's salt-encrusted ears. One night,
another squall, icicles hanging from everywhere, my father said, a huge wave, gray-
tipped, sharp as steel, washed that parrot overboard, never to be seen again.
In the hot pink of dawn, every crewman woke and gathered, having been called
From their small two-bunk caverns, hanging their heads, caps doffed, and every
     man
cried, suddenly aware of only the sound of the sea around them. The captain died
the next year, on land, where he hated being. Did I tell you, my father said, through
lips cracked by thirst, in his hospital bed, scrotum and stomach swollen by cancer,
inoperable, untreatable, some faceless doctor said, did I tell you, I was in the
     Ardennes,
during the Battle of the Bulge, how cold it was, my toes froze hard, my fingers
still hurt when I remember, artillery shells exploding in the trees, splinters raining
all over us in our foxholes, and what a foot-long sliver of wood looks like
sticking out of a man's head? It was where I won the Bronze Star, for having been
     there,
by accident, not knowing those gray men in their pure-white snow suits would
     come
silently from among those dead trees. Then he slept.

Dredging up
A Puerto Rican city kid's time on a Long Island truck farm

That summer, last on that farm, I went out into what any poet would call
golden light, one morning, out to take a look at the pigs that were mine
to care for, some fat, some sleek, or old or young, past where the hens
still slept, and under the shade of a tree that has turned into shadow in
my recollecting, my reaching deep and pulling each item in this memory
up, putting that day together again, the mucilage for it the wanting to go
back to when I was that age. Under that tree is where the pig pen stood,
close by the house, and I carried apples—I don't know from where they came—
to throw one to each of them, waking the ones that slept, the ones awake
coming to get their share, and I had no idea when I was a boy, that pigs
were aware, were more than sources of chops, or the amusement their squeals
brought, those funny sounds, when they realized they were going to die,
throats cut, bled out. There was one pig I loved, and in remembering him,
or her, that pig has become a pink smudge, a smear, I can't resolve. I
loved that pig, and if I am not making this up, every day on that farm
my godfather owned, where my family went every summer for two weeks,
I climbed into that pen and sat in shit and mud, and pulled that pig to me,
to kiss it and hug it, going afterwards inside, after having stripped
to my underwear, to sneak into the shower, to throw those clothes among
others worn to do farm work. That last day, when my father and mother
packed what we had brought, my god father chose one pig to kill,
to cut its throat, to slit it open, emptying it of heart and lungs, the other
parts I had no knowledge of, then, to be placed on a spit and turned
all day long, until done, we might sit down to eat. Not me. I recall
how, hearing that squeal, I looked to see my pig gone, and, later, a pig
on a spit that looked like any dead pig, and how I would not sit to eat,
staying inside, and how every summer thereafter, I would not go
to that farm where morning light had always seemed.

Encomium for my dead mother

There have been so many night since her death, before I've gone to bed, or
already in it, before sleep, I've wondered what it must have been like to have been
her, the making of her children, her woman parts I prefer not to think about,

breast-feeding, the sensation of that, the constant housework, washing socks
and underwear by hand, then hanging everything cleaned on a clothesline outside
of her kitchen window, the hours spent at her stove, and how she put

dishes together, measuring nothing, everything by eye. I wonder what it was like
for her to have gotten up while it was dark, to rouse each child, shepherding us
from bed to bathroom to kitchen table for soft-boiled eggs, oatmeal, glasses of

cold milk, our eyes half-closed, her going back and forth, laying clothing out
and making sure we had our shoes lined up just right, ready to put on, for her
to walk us to our school four blocks away, waiting for our lines to form, for us

to go in, nuns in black all around us. And, those nights, I've wondered what
it must have been like for her to have turned from our school's closing doors,
to have gone to the sweatshop where she went, to sew buttons onto clothes, one

penny for each button sewn on just right, nothing for those attached all wrong,
dim light coming in through windows never washed since the Italians and
the Irish sat in those same chairs, bent over, sewing and sewing. I've wondered what

she must have thought about, fingers pricked by slipping needles, each drop
of blood, joining others on the floor, generations of them, and how deftly
her fingers must have moved, earning one by one, penny after penny.

What precedes the composition of a coda

Not in the crowded steerage holds dressed in European tatters
but dressed in second-hand American fashions ten years
out of date, they came on the cheap midnight flights I once wrote
when twenty-two or three and I had long hair then, springy
from African blood at its roots, and my cheekbones were
covered with taut skin, were high and protruded like
the cheek bones of the Taino people whose bones still lie
beneath jungle mulch, thick carpet of rotting branches and leaves.
Young and unafraid and thin, and, so I thought, pretty, someone
whose bare skin glimmered, I sat overlooking Harvard Square
and wrote in pencil on legal pads, in what seems like eons
before the advent of computers. Those men I wrote about
went *into the sleeping foreign cities, men with their pockets*
stuffed full of contraband dreams is what I wrote, and did not
either think or dream of more than that kind of flight, not
from hovels in tropical air to hovels made of chipped brick
in air that froze every six months, but of how the hand
that held a No. 2 pencil would still be writing, for more
than fifty years.

My parent's house goes up for sale

Our mother's dead, our father, home emptied of everything
they once had—old sofa with its plastic slipcovers yellowed
and cracked from children who came to visit and sat and ate

on TV trays every dish placed before them, the rice, the beans,
the ripe plantains cut at a slant and fried just right, becoming
gold and black, and slices of avocado lightly salted, pork chops

that didn't need any light to glisten, giving off a radiance. We
ate and laughed and rose, pushing those TV trays aside and went
to where our mother, in the kitchen, old and bent by age, bent

over dishes in the sink, one eye on the stove, the next meal
being cooked, and out to where my father imitated a storm cloud,
all swirling black, slumped into his easy chair, alone, with no one

within a certain circumference, son or daughter briefly swooping
in, to plant a kiss on his bald head, a hair here or there, wiry, gray
sticking up. Those nights aren't in the realtor's pictures of living

room, of kitchen, of dining area where no one sat to eat, or rooms
where beds always lay rumpled and unmade, sheets coated with
sweat and dander, of our father, our mother, of children when

they came, of grandchildren, rooms empty of those childrens'
shouts and laughter. And, the old pile carpet shampooed and washed,
cleaned of grime, of foot prints worn into them, trails incised

over the years of mother and father going about what they did, of
sons and daughters, of grandchildren in their hordes.

It's always a long journey to find any kind of love

That was very sweet you say
when I hand over a three-dollar rose
I bought

down at the local supermarket
on my way to find you
sitting in a chair, in a restaurant

where the chef is known
for the excellence of his cooking,
for how deftly his hands

move across chopping boards
while he heaps
abuse on the help, and how

he can be heard
through doors that swing
open and shut as waiters

pass through them, with
the clarity and predictability
of metronomes. I blushed

when you said
the word *sweet,* at how
your lashes

swept down and up again,
catching candle light, light
from bulbs in their sconces

and how I joined your sense
of what had transpired
within you

when I handed over that rose,
bringing it from
behind my back, by looking

down at my feet, kept out of sight
so you might not see
how worn my shoes were,

those digits beneath
that old leather, those
twenty-six bones, from having

had to cope with Zeno's Paradox,
never thinking
I might actually arrive.

IV.

Reading the signs

The astrological charts all say I'm triple fire sign, the moon in this,
the sun in that, Jupiter off somewhere on its own, spinning dizzily
while its atmosphere sings some crazy baritone tune no one
can figure out. Who knows what Saturn might be doing
during all of this. For good measure throw in Neptune, promote
Pluto back to planet status so it can also exert a greater influence
on my small trajectory through what's been called space/time
where I do my own rapid spinning while trying to understand,
well, anything at all, how it's come to what it's come to, this
small and finite life, though this concept of mortality, that some day
I won't be here anymore, in front of a computer, or in my bed
tossing and turning at three in the morning, long, ropy strings
of dreams and hopes slithering around somewhere inside my brain,
that is something I can't quite wrap my arms or head around.
What does that mean? Last week, at my sister-in-law's funeral,
fifty-six and gnawed to nothing by pancreatic cancer, she didn't
look anything like what I remembered. She became all dried
stretched skin. Where was she? I looked into the box,
and saw very little left. What good is any horoscope if
what is set down as destiny and blazes from the page
when we are utterly lost in fantasies of fabulous futures, wealth,
(maybe), sex (we hope), ongoing good looks, health and well-being
all of those things, and more, will vanish in a hospital. The only
metaphor I can think of to describe what she went through,
and everyone else I know who wound up dead, either too young,
or old and tired, is being flushed. Perhaps we are like the phenomenon
of black holes, aptly named singularities, places where on the other
side of an event horizon, where particles too small to be perceived,
blaze and are transformed by that crossing over into what is
presently inexplicable. Or, maybe not. Maybe that isn't the case.
All I know, right now, here, on a tepid summer day, with wan light
streaming through my dusty window, is that I am sitting, erect
in my desk chair, aware, nerve by nerve, of what presses against
my physical body, and that I am a locus into which this world,
what little of it I see, for now streams in.

A minor and parenthetical notation to what will later occur

Tonight's
the night. No more rehearsing or nursing a part is what came to mind,

when
this morning, my eyes opened and, first thing, I thought

of
your thighs and eyes, of your blond hair, smooth as any silk,

the sheer
satin sheet of your ass, and how tonight, you and I will ride

each
other for several hours, while your neighbors' voices drift through

your
open window and your cat cowers in the doorway. Do not go

gentle
into that good night
is a strange turn of phrase to pair

with
the theme song from Bugs Bunny's defunct show, from when

we
were children and never thought of old age and death, as tonight

we
will so vehemently deny our mortality by taking our clothing off,

doffing
that which hides the rills and depressions in our flesh, while we pretend

to
be immortal enough that what we do will be repeated over

and
over again, from week to week, no end in sight to what we do at night

when
the moon's slipped behind gray clouds, and the heater

in
your room comes on.

Parenting

Last night, I dreamt my son waited for me
on the moon, holding his breath, his skin
turning gray, his cheeks ballooned, his eyes
tightly shut. I dreamt I rose from my bed,
that I grew wings, long, feathery and white,
with which to fly through the atmosphere,
which I did, pinions beating strongly, sensations
I'd never felt before, arms spread. I laughed
as I rose, for as long as there was air, for
as long as I could, shutting my mouth as I
rose to where blue turned black and the earth's
gorgeous curve became more apparent. I flew,
wings folded behind me, against my back, arms
at my sides, face pointed to that orb, shining
and so far, going faster all of the time, flying
as I had always imagined flying would be.
I covered the distance in no time at all, it seemed,
and looked behind me as I went, watching
my home planet become smaller, and did not feel
any pang of regret to have left it. Landing,
I went to where my son knelt, as if in prayer,
forehead in lunar dust, that smudged it
as I lifted him. Holding him tightly to my chest,
I leaped and went the way I'd come, seeing
earth grow, its seas sparkling, its lands so brown
and green, and did not look back to the moon.
Into the atmosphere again, I inhaled when we
were low enough, and I said to my son
that he should breathe, draw breath in, which
he did, gasping, chest swelling so much, I felt
it pushing against my breast, and I woke, going
to the window to look out, still feeling his weight
in my arms, his heft.

Experience attendant to living in a townhouse

What are those strange noises coming from the parking lot, late,
when all I am trying to do is sleep, burrowing into the mattress,
so I may fade from this world into another, so I may escape age
and distress, terror and grief by becoming my most beautiful self.
Nights, I try to pretend the mattress, that sags in its middle, making
my back hurt when I wake, is a womb, dried out from disuse, that
I, going more deeply into it, may rehydrate that shelter, that lovely
sanctuary, where the portents dark carry are good ones, and not
what we usually associate with a lack of sight. As I begin that drift,
as I begin to become sodden and sink, I imagine, or try to remember,
going back to that when, what it must be like for a developing baby,
brain just formed and sparking as it works, to have its eyes shut, for
it to float as it does, what it imagines, given that it only experiences
limited stimuli, hands folded against its chest, legs pushed up
by its limited space, the indicators of its gender just developing.
My old mattress holds me, the sheets I've spread across it and left
for weeks, because I sleep alone, hold me like a gloved palm, the slivers
of the self I've sloughed off, dead skin, flake after flake that serves
to feed creatures so little, the magnitude of what they do overwhelms
the self that remains. All night long, human hooting in the parking lot.
Are they drunk? I hear car doors slam, listen to chuckles as people,
male or female, alight and make their way to their own beds,
Are their mattresses for them what mine is to me, a refuge, a place
in which to briefly hide, a space, on those nights when my dreams align
with an interpretation of what this stuffed creation of cotton and springs
means, a palm that holds me up to the sky, the radiation that comes
from light years away, or my mother reaching from wherever she is,
to hold me within her, as she once did.

On the overnight massacre in an Orlando FL nightclub

Dance, and while you dance, dream of smooth cheeks, your face
pressed against them after this night is over, but, for now, under
spinning lights, watch the body with which you dance move, how
sleek it is, how sleek your partner's, how easily your limbs bend,
and, as you move into the arms of the someone you love, with who
you will sleep after all the dancing is done, allow your mind to wander
to the love you will make, the different dance of clothing coming off,
the movement of your love, how your legs will entwine, for some,
for the first time, for others all around you, making love, when
it is late, and they are tired, will be a repeated melody, their voices,
in their homes, shaping a chorus that changes all the time. Move
and dance, weave yourself through the music to which you dance,
into the body of the one who dances with you. Close your eyes.
Dream and dance. Dance the dream. Dream and dance and weave
until last call, until this evening ends.

Every night a new beginning

Big Bang is what I dream about
some nights when erotic fantasies

have dried up and nothing
else comes along, the dead

I loved and love tired of being called
from the basement room

of my consciousness to pirouette
in front of me

in what they wore last, mouths
sealed against

speaking, not wanting to witness
anymore my arms stretched

out to them I cannot reach.
Big Bang, primordial molecule

so small in
my dreaming it is the tiniest

but fiercest glow, an incandescence
beyond believing, expanding

into the everything
I ever wanted to know.

[The old lady never sat down]

The old lady almost never sat down, and, when she did,
it was hard for her to get up by herself, looking up

for god's strong hand to reach down, like in cartoons,
from inside of a cloud, the rest of him hidden, to grip

her old hand, not hard, but tenderly, and to lift her,
making her feel for just a moment as if she was, again,

a young woman starting out as wife and mother. Once up,
she moved, old legs aching is what she said, but she had

to keep moving, always more to do, always food to cook
and, after, dishes to wash, her old legs like metronomes

slowing down, until one day, she said she knew, they would
no longer move back and forth, propelling her with speed

diminishing from kitchen to living room to laundry room
to where an old broom stood, an old dust pan, in a corner

into which she would go, lost in shadow, to later, and slowly,
emerge, to move across her living room, and on and on and on.

Waiting
> *After Joyce Sutphen*

He does what he does
and what his father did, the same routine—

early to rise
after a sleepless night

of tossing and turning
and getting up to pee

when the urge becomes
too powerful to resist, followed by

a tour of every wall, flashlight in hand,
looking at pictures of long ago,

a time when all of his loves

were little or loved him back, alive
or now dead and buried, turned

into unimaginable husks, as is
the past to which

he calls
those nights when roaming halls

and wandering through rooms
is all he now knows how to do,

careful not to stub his toes, careful
not to step in

whatever mess
a geriatric cat has unintentionally made.

The migrants before they came

When it came time to cross, before the sun was fully up, all of us lined up,
single file and walked out and along a path that descended at an angle,
ground beneath our feet still firm, if bumpy, its clumps of grass tripping
us as we walked along, moving low-hanging branches aside, amazed
at how cool mornings were, how wet those branches felt, and the air
itself, and said nothing to each other, but listened to the breeze, to
birds we could not see as we went, to insects somewhere, all around us,
front, behind. We walked, carrying our rucksacks, or burlap bags
filled with what little we cared to carry forward with us through time
until it was time to discard a pair of shoes, or to repurpose the one
sock we might have left of a pair, or turn into a rag to wipe clean
some grimy surface a pair of ripped and worn-through underwear.
We moved, not caring to be silent, but being silent in the way
we moved along, the occasional stumble of someone in back or in front.
one of us muttering under his or her breath. We moved and came
to that place where water met land, a muddy bank where land
and water became confused about what was what, mud that was
thick a black coming up around our ankles, cold mud that felt to us
to be good, and we stood and looked out over that water, the color
of it, the speed at which it moved, the ripples across its top, the way
light already glinted from it, seeming to us as if someone with
a mirror was signaling to us in a language we did not comprehend.

Panegyric for my youngest son

Elliot, now six, is busy becoming himself, humming like a hive.
He reads random signs, puzzling out polysyllabic words, saying

them backwards so he can play with their sound. He sits
on his father's lap, legs already touching floor, leaning back,

his head, with him inside of it, already becomes a mystery.
Against his father's chest, right hand held up to stroke his father's

cheek, his sparse beard, the kind older men grow to disguise
how the architecture of the jaw has become weak, he sings,

having learned words to songs his father's never heard, hearing
a song one time, and knowing it throughout, voice still

a little boy's voice, high and reedy and flat, not able to carry
more than a rudimentary tune, no hint, no trace of how that voice

will change forever in a few years. He watches Youtube videos
while his father kisses the back of his head, offering analysis

and commentary on video games, scary ones, he loves, rattling on,
saying whatever comes into his mind, asking the meaning of words

he doesn't know, that quickly go into the growing catalog beneath
the bones of his small skull, where who he is and will become

is nestled, looking out. When his father takes him home, where he
and his mother live, he says *Pick me up daddy Pick me up* rising into air,

hugging and being hugged, and having hugged, immediately runs off.

Expiation Exorcism Expurgation
For DCC

I have come to sit in one old chair in an empty room, painted white,
and lit by natural light coming through a skylight, at what appears to be
midday, so that I will not have to also deal with night's peregrinations
of plangent shadows intruding into the anywhere where I might be.
I have come in through a door that promptly disappeared and have listened
to the way my soft sneakers slid against a parquet floor made to gleam,
and have found the company of small echoes to be comforting to me,
and have sat, gingerly at first, on the edge of that wooden chair, one
worn smooth by repeated use, by who I have no idea, perhaps, other men,
like me, who come in diffidently and have sat and have thought
it might be more appropriate to kneel, perhaps to have rent their clothing,
or to have entered with their thick or sparse hair already covered with
fine ash scooped from fireplaces. There, in that brightly lit space, in
an old chair polished and made to gleam by the restless movements
of those who have sat in it, I have carefully placed myself, hands resting
on my knees, listening for whatever murmuration, whatever small noise,
of my joints cracking, or the tiny heave of lungs inhaling and expelling air,
of my heart, no longer placid, no longer thought durable and eternal
in its operation, and have spoken out loud, though beginning in a tone
more hushed than bold, to no one but one of the four walls I've faced,
recounting what I have spent years cataloging, a long list added to
and revised every day immediately after waking, erasures, strike-outs,
modifications and embellishments, as well as footnotes where they
were appropriate, a lengthening list, a recitation on paper of everything
done wrong, every mistake made, every error in judgment, every willful
commission of hurtful acts, every deliberate act, of omission or not.
I have come to shed the chrysalis I have worn, the hard carapace I have
kept on, day and night, that shell no one could penetrate where I have
cowered, hiding within it, as if that outside that imitated the who of who
I am was more real than what was within it, febrile and soft, tender, bruised,
knocked to whatever floor or ground, left exhausted, not broken but
growing more aware, until the desire to crack my way out of it, and rise,
new and wet, has overcome. I have come into an empty room filled
with light coming in, where the walls are bare and white, seeming to gleam
as I look at them, in a chair burnished over and over, to where
you are not, nor will ever be again, to open my mouth, to speak, allowing

whatever miasmas have accrued out to form and float, to dissipate,
to disappear, not as if they had never been, but had finally been thrown up
and out, before falling to my knees, forehead resting on that room's floor.

Leaving Spanish behind for my true love

Que quiere decir la palabra Chifle, que, contemplando
lo que quiere decir me caigo, entonces, into English
where I am more comfortable, where I can easily discern
the meaning of most words, unlike, in Spanish, I struggle
to swim and seem natural at speaking in that language,
enunciating as clearly as I am able so I don't seem
like someone who's come from its outside.
I try, I do, to dream in the language of my forebears,
to see as they saw the universe through the medium
of that tongue, and find that I can't, waking in night
to say whatever I want to say in the tongue of the conqueror,
a language I love so madly, I spend hours writing in it,
in front of my computer, fingers clacking along
in the dance most natural to my language, the one
I take in every time I listen to the radio or watch TV,
what's come out of the harsh and crackling syllables
of old Anglo-Saxon, mine now, mine, all mine, this
tongue, this way of shaping and perceiving in which
I live, morning, noon, night, all of the time, always.

To those future men who will be named Carlos

After Eleanor Ross Taylor

Some of you will Salsa dance yourselves
across whatever future rooms you will happen to be in,
and some will do an old-fashioned 1950's I-am-too-cool
ditty bop down an inner-city street, and some
will be four-eyed young men wanting nothing more
than to inhabit the stacks of whatever public library is
blocks from where you live with your blue-collar parents,
and some of you will unrelentingly play with yourselves
late at night, beneath your thin covers, flashlights in one hand,
and some, walking down a boulevard will stop to look
at a malnourished city tree, bent over by too much pollution
coating its few leaves, and you will stop and you will wonder
why there is being as opposed to not.

A flash on previous visits to Tampa in Florida now that my parents are dead

Grass of a different sort than I am used to, broad-bladed, growing
apart from other blades of its kind, concealing snakes and really big
spiders that scuttle as they do in movies, and frogs just come from
their tadpole stage, soaking up rain quickly, sandy soil, not thick
and dark brown loam, or even the potting soil to which I am used
to seeing, or running my fingers through. Everything there not
the same as here, even the people whose spindly legs are always
being shown, bared to skies too blue to be true, to water whose
saline content reminds me of, when I go into it, of beginnings,
of something really small coalescing and breaking itself into another
of itself, a process, an inauguration. All of this comes back to me
when I stop, suddenly, wherever I may be walking, down a store aisle,
or even down my hall seeking whatever room, to be alone with
grief or joy. I have found either one will do, to open my mouth
and to have issue from it one of two kinds of cries, variations in
the way they sound, at times, almost indistinguishable, prompting
me to wonder if I am happy or sad, especially when a recliner scoops
me into it, and I sink, holding my breath as if sinking into the waters
of the Atlantic, about which I am about to begin to think, as said,
of saline content, of buoyancy, of having gone down to that ocean
for a day of picnic food, of salt itch after immersion, of those who
came with me, there, to have all of our feet burned by white sand
before returning to the lawn of my parents' old house, where that
strange grass, whose name I never learned, poked skyward, whatever
was in it scattering as our car doors slammed.

Aubade #303-F

Come dawn and I briefly wake, bleary and sore, feeling strange
because light's arrival's dim, as if most of it's been delayed, is
coming late or later still, and what I hear, window cracked
to allow a breeze to have entered while I slept, is neighbors
who work too hard and come home bent and worn to slivers,
getting to their cars to begin their long days of filling trucks
with items to be delivered, to stand on rooftops, at a slant,
nails gripped by teeth, hands curved around hammers. I stir
and move, throwing covers off, pulling them back over me, so I
may seek to fade again, becoming sepia, and lighter as I fade
back into my private realm, where I am young and can do
anything I choose. Some nights, I fly, everyone does, defying
the tug of jealous ground, to hold me down, as if in a bear hug.
Others, I make love all night along, old lovers come back
filled with forgiveness and desire, When done, we speak as we
once could, and laugh. I wake and push my covers off and seek
to stand, finding equilibrium to be relearned, the tottering from
side to side, as if at sea, a gentle swell, my refusal to reach out
to place a hand against a wall. I am not old. Not yet. Nor weak.

Carlos Martinez is sixty-seven years old, and was born and raised in the Spanish Harlem neighborhood of New York City, where he attended his local parish elementary school, and graduated from Haaren High School. He attended Trinity College in Hartford CT, from which he graduated with a BA in Philosophy. He began writing poetry at the age of sixteen, encouraged and helped by his high school English Honors teacher. He had a long and varied career in both the private non-profit sector and government, finally leaving government to obtain his MFA in Creative Writing at the age of forty-eight. Since the acquisition of his graduate degree, he has taught composition, various literature and creative writing courses at a variety of schools: Highline and Green River Community Colleges, Western Washington University and, most recently, at Northwest Indian College. He has published extensively in a variety of local and national literary journals and anthologies, and has had three chapbooks published by Finishing Line Press. This is his first full-length collection. In addition, he has read at many venues in the Seattle and Bellingham areas, has twice been a reader at the Skagit River Poetry Festival, has been a featured reader at Gonzaga and Willamette Universities and at Trinity College, his alma mater. He has also read at the Grolier and Open Books Bookstores, two of three poetry-only bookstores in the country. He is presently at work on a new full-length collection he hopes to have published.